THE PROJECT
Happiness

A PRACTICAL APROACH IN REAL WORLD

PARTEEK TRIPATHI

The project happiness by Prateek Tripathi

Table of Contents

About the book

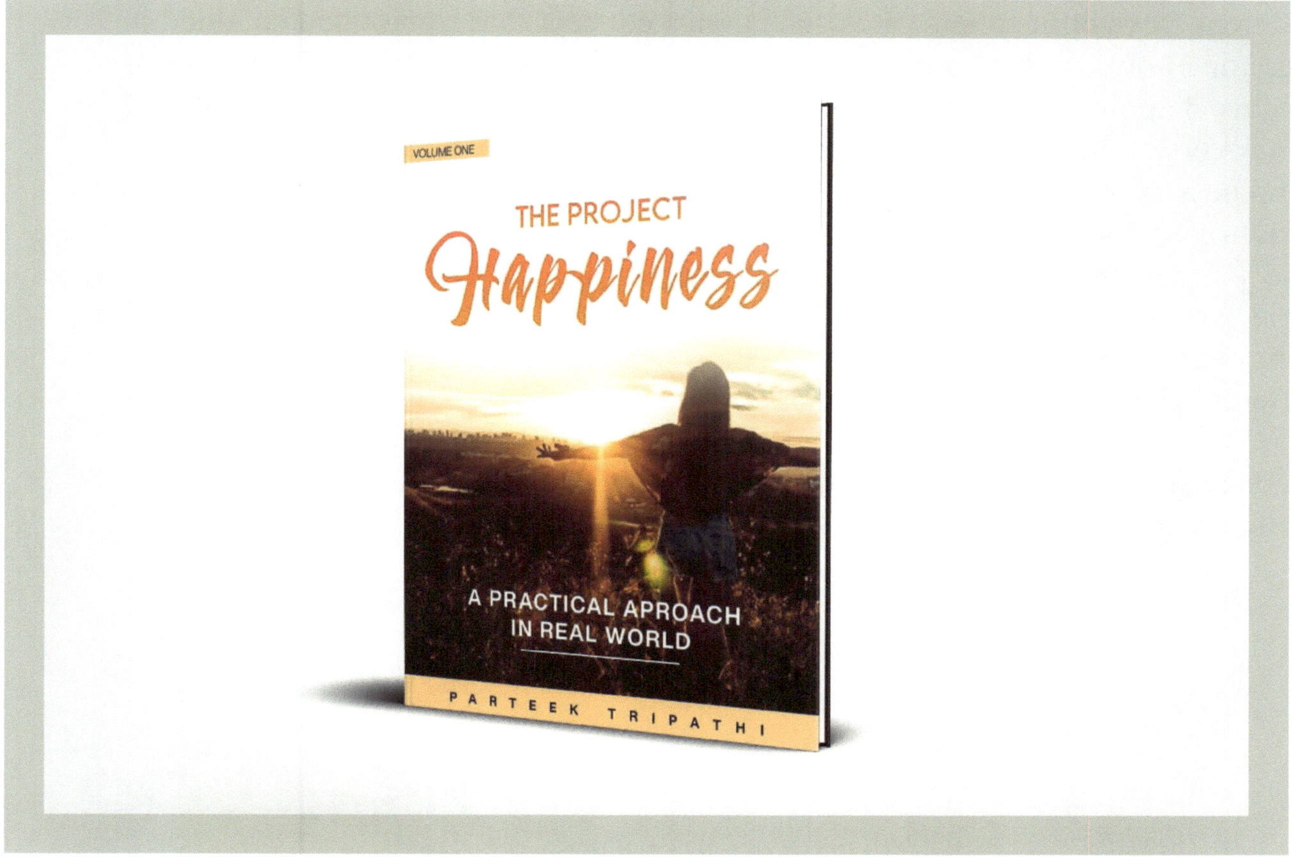

In this book, according to the author happiness is not something that can be found in the outside world, one has to search within very deeply and thoroughly to find it. This book totally depends upon real life experiences. The ancient techniques will be unveiled and also their respective use in the modern life of every human beings which will go on further in various volumes. "The happiness project" – volume1 you will see a mirror that will be helpful to see your own shadow. The most important thing is to enjoy your life—to be happy—it's all that matters. You cannot protect yourself from sadness without protecting yourself from happiness.

INTRODUCTION

So after studying the reasons and perceptions about happiness in different cultures and ethnicity and trying to understand the essence it is really hard for me to describe the true meaning and the ways to achieve happiness in so many different ways on manners , it is such a vast concept that cannot be contained in mere one book at all , I am still searching and studying the ways and bridges to achieve happiness in one way or another. As I said this is a very vast and controversial topic, I will try to elaborate my thinking, and what is real happiness in different cultural and spiritual ways ancient and modern in this series of books, because one is not big enough to grasp the concept so easily.
The journey that you about to start with me through this first volume in the series of this book is going to be maybe astonishing, enlightening or maybe very controversial as I stated earlier, we will be researching about the topic in every different genre and in very unique and interesting ways.

So once again thank you for taking your interest an I pray that
You may get the answers that you are looking for through this series.

How not to worry about money?

If there's something that stresses people out, it's financial problems.

On March 11th, 2020, the coronavirus outbreak was officially declared a pandemic.

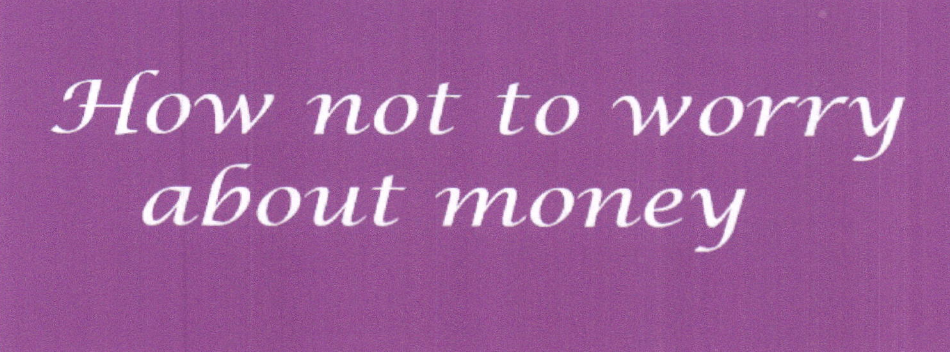

COVID-19 not only started to threaten people's health on a global scale; it also severely affected the economy.

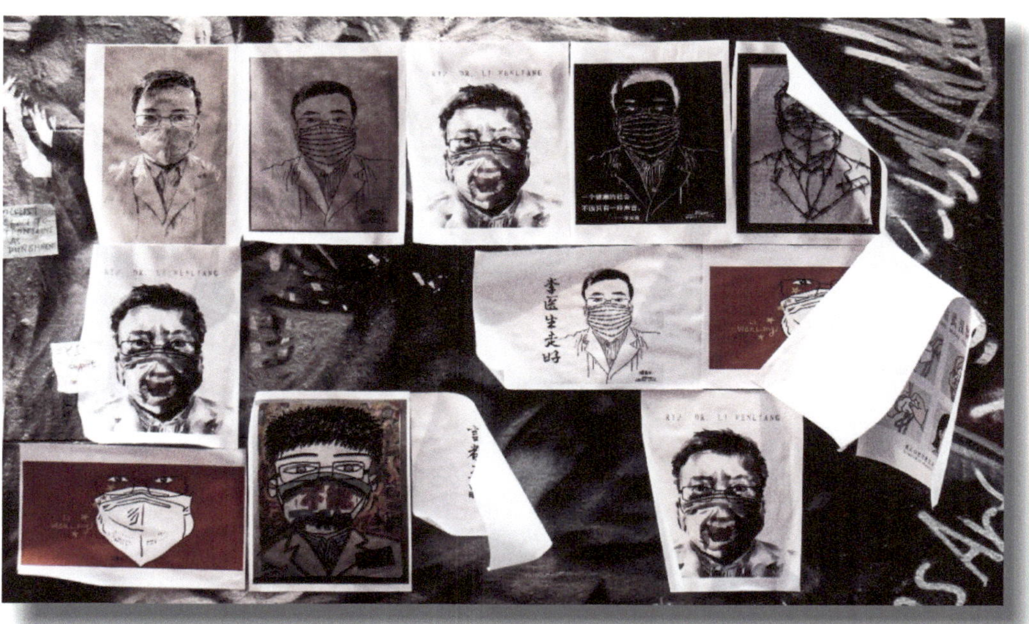

When you're laid off by your company, or your business has to shut down, or this crisis damages your finances in any other way, there's a likelihood that you're struggling to make ends meet. Money problems often cause anxiety, because they are a direct threat to our sense of self-preservation.

1. What if I have no income?
2. What if I become poor?
3. What's going to happen next?

In this chapter, I'd like to share six Stoic teachings that will not solve your money problems directly but might help you to change your perspective, regain your focus and tranquillity,
and get through financially difficult times.

Chapter 1

Get back to basics

The ancient Stoics were masters at observing human nature and the nature of reality.
Being closely related to the Cynic school, they didn't put too much value on material wealth. Time, for them, was the greatest commodity.
And our ability to choose and act, they saw as much more valuable than any amount of money will ever be.
Wealth surely is nice, but not only is it beyond our control: it isn't necessary to be happy either. To survive, we need food and shelter.
And for the majority of the world's population, even in the poor regions of the world, such as our country this bare minimum is available.

If you've got access to Internet, then you probably have your basic needs met.
But for many people, this isn't enough. Especially in developed countries, there's so much more to money besides it being a way
to pay for survival.
We might want to ask ourselves:

Why are we so attached to our current income?
Why can't we do, at least temporarily, with less?
Is it because we want to keep up with the Jones's?
Do we have a social circle that attaches a lot of importance to status?
Perhaps we are afraid to lose our spouse if we fail to keep our wealth intact?

"Fidelity purchased with money, money can destroy," Stoic philosopher Seneca once wrote.

Here's another example to keep in mind:

"Suppose that you hold wealth to be a good: poverty will then distress you, and, which is most pitiable, it will be an imaginary poverty. For you may be rich, and nevertheless, because your neighbour is richer, you suppose yourself to be poor exactly by the same amount in which you fall short of your neighbour."

Seneca (Moral Letters to Lucilius),104-9

Anything that goes beyond survival is basically obsolete.

It's nice to have status, for example, but according to Stoic philosophy, we must be willing to give that up, if that's the price we pay for tranquillity.

Chapter 2

Focus on what we can influence

There's no single worry in the world that can stop bad things from happening. Yet, when we're struggling financially, we're often immersed in the future, and try to control things that we have no power over.

Our greatest fear might be losing our money, and not being able to pay the bills. But not having money doesn't take away the strongest tool we have, which is our ability to act.
Taking action doesn't happen in the past, nor does it happen in the future.
It happens exclusively in the present.

The present is where the future is made.
Therefore, worrying is not only a complete waste of time: it's detrimental to our ability to act when we should.
Instead of staring at a long, endless road of obstacles, we can compartmentalize our undertakings and focus on the task at hand.
Only what we can change, right now, is what counts.

Chapter 3

Ask for help

The Stoics observed that everything nature comes up with has a part in the play. We're all in this together, and by helping each other out in difficult times we act in the benefit of the whole.

Looking at the way people behave during a crisis, like the COVID-19 crisis, for example, we can conclude that human nature has an inclination to help a fellow human out.

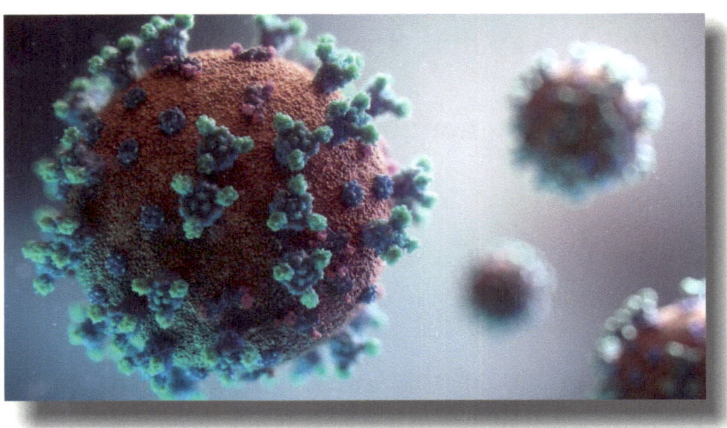

Moreover, there's a lot of research indicating that helping people makes you happy. In his Meditations, Marcus Aurelius wrote that we shouldn't be afraid to ask each other for help.

"Don't be ashamed to need help.
Like a soldier storming a wall, you have a mission to accomplish.
And if you've been wounded and you need a comrade to pull you up?
So what?"
-Marcus Aurelius (Meditations), 7-7

When we look at the nature of the universe, we'll discover that everything is interconnected.
We depend on our surroundings; on the oxygen we breathe, on the powerplant that supplies our homes with electricity, on the people that pick up our trash, and so on. Refusing to ask for help in an interdependent world is kind of insane.

Chapter 4

Remember that you're not alone

If you're at least a bit wealthy, then you set yourself apart from an enormous group of people.
Especially in Western Europe, there's such a strong social safety net, that it takes quite some hardships and bad luck to become truly poor.
No matter where you're from, your financial struggles could lead to the loss of wealth. This is what scares people.

The biggest fear of the wealthy is the fear to lose it all.

Seneca, for example, was quite hung up on themes like 'wealth' and 'poverty'. As a rich statesman, he was aware of the burden that the rich bear, which is that what you have, you can lose.

But so he thought: "I may become a poor man; I shall then be one among many."

When you look at it from a wider perspective, you'll see that you're far from alone when you struggle financially. So many people live in poverty, so many live pay check to pay check.

So, you might lose your wealth, but then you'll share your troubles with many souls.

Chapter 5

Put your tranquillity first

Stoic philosopher Epictetus was very clear about this: "your peace of mind is more important than outside affairs."

Yet, when we're struggling financially, we often let external circumstances decide our mood.
This doesn't mean that we shouldn't try to improve our financial situation; it means that from a human point of view we have to set our priorities straight.
Looking for work, doubling down on our business, finding ways to make money on the side: there's nothing wrong with that.
As long as we don't sacrifice our mental wellbeing:

"If you want to improve, reject such reasonings as these: "If I neglect my affairs, I'll
have no income; if I don't correct my servant, he will be bad."
For it is better to die with hunger, exempt from grief and fear, than to live in affluence
with perturbation; and it is better your servant should be bad, than you unhappy."
-   Epictetus (Enchiridion), 12

This may seem a bit unrealistic and extreme, but since the Stoics value time more than anything, they'd argue that we should always aim to be happy under any circumstances. A simple method that modern Stoics use to make peace with an uncertain future is 'amor fati'. This Latin phrase means 'love of fate'. Amor fati is the practice of embracing the future, regardless of the outcome. We will discuss about it in different chapter in this book.

Chapter 6

Remember what you do have

Lastly, we tend to overlook the things we have and focus on the things we haven't. This is probably because we take so many things for granted, that we actually forget how blessed we are.

Marcus Aurelius teaches us to ignore what we don't have, and try to imagine what it's like to don't have what we actually have:

"Look at what you have, the things you value most, and think of how much
you'd crave
them if you didn't have them.
But be careful.
Don't feel such satisfaction that you start to overvalue them, that it would upset
you
to lose them."
-   Marcus Aurelius (Meditations), 7-27

In simple words in order to be happy first we have to learn being thankful and start having some gratitude for whatever we possess, in terms of our body mind and finances even if it's not enough in the eyes of the world, There's much

more to life besides money. Your healthy your body, your relationships, your freedom.
But the most important thing we possess is our ability to choose.
In any given situation, we have the power to choose how we deal with it.
And that's priceless.

Art of not trying

Those who stand on tiptoes do not stand firmly.
Those who rush ahead don't get very far.
Those who try to outshine others dim their own light
- Lao Tzu

How can we improve when we stop trying to improve?
Many people waste their efforts trying to better their lives with questionable results. They gain knowledge and chase external things while exhausting their bodies, and burdening their minds - only to end up in discontent.
Many spiritual Masters observed that humans tend to act in ways that are counterproductive. And in their attempts to alter the natural way, they only make things worse. All these strivings, rules, ethics, values, surely are invented to benefit humanity. But according to the ancient sages, we should get rid of them all. Why?
Because all these manmade ideas only remove us further from the natural flow of life.

 Trying to alter what nature has intended, is like swimming against the stream: it's exhausting and gets us nowhere.
Behind the ever-changing universe lies a mysterious and undefinable force that the Taoists call 'Tao', The Hindus call it 'Prana', the source of creation, there

are many names to it. The 'Tao' or the 'source of creation', is all-encompassing, and it's beyond everything that our senses can perceive.
Still, we can know and feel the 'Tao', even though we cannot comprehend it.
This symbolizes the tragic attempts by humans to conceptualize things that are beyond their understanding.
We use names, categories, we select and discern, but fail to grasp what the universe is truly like.
So, we create a deception; an artifice that makes life understandable for humans.
But by trying to comprehend, we lose the connection from the source.

Chapter 7
The Tragedy of Trying

"Five colours blind the eye.
Five notes deafen the ear.
Five flavours make the palate go stale,"
- Lao Tzu (Tao Te Ching.)

So, by arranging colours, notes, and flavours, we might enhance our understanding, but we also limit it, as there's so much more outside of these fixed concepts.

The same goes for the human tendency to make rock-solid rules for everything, to get a sense of control.
Again, we limit ourselves by doing so because the world is ever-changing, and what works today, may not work tomorrow.
Also, from a sense of solidarity and justice, people create immense bodies of ethics, moral codes, and rituals, that form an artificial way of life.
Even though the intentions are good: they try to make things work while building their own prisons. Now, let's talk about the word 'trying'.
I think most of us are familiar with the idea that we should simply 'act' and not 'try'. This idea is closely related to the 'flow-state'.
In a flow-state one becomes the act, like a dancer who becomes the dance, or the poet who becomes the poem. This is wu wei, a concept that can be literally

translated as 'non-doing' or 'doing nothing'. In the context of the flow state, wu wei translates best as 'effortless action', because we act in a smooth and painless manner.
In the context of this book, however, translating wu wei as 'non-doing' or 'doing nothing' fits best.

Literally 'doing nothing' is often seen as unproductive, and as a useless way of being, in which there's no progression.

But according to the Taoists and many other spiritual masters, nothing is further from the truth. When we keep in mind that the universe is in flux and in a state of entropy, we'll realize that there's always progression in the natural flow of life. So instead of using force, and exhausting ourselves (which is the favourite method of today's culture), we could travel through life much more easily by using intelligence.

Because isn't it so, that so many times, problems seem to solve themselves?
And that by 'taking action' we often make things worse?
When we waste our time trying to improve things, we distance ourselves from the natural course. We repeatedly act in ways that are (according to the Taoists) unnatural and waste our bodies

and minds doing so. So, why do we do this?
Well, it has a lot to do with how we attribute value to certain things.
For example, when we're averse to poverty, but desire money and fame, and when we're averse to being lonely but desire to be part of something.
So we try to eradicate the former, and increase the latter, while the latter cannot exist without the former.
Also, we think that it's necessary to conform and alter nature based on certain belief systems. We try to better the world, while the results of our interventions are kind of questionable.

Chapter 8

How We Try

Now, how can we bring these ancient theories into the modern world?
According to Taoist thinking, in what ways do we, modern humans, 'try', while our efforts only leave us with peanuts in the end?
Let's explore some examples of how we 'try', by exploring some ancient scriptures.
The first one is…

Trying to improve the world

Alan Watts, who was a fervent scholar of Taoism, once pointed out that the goodie-goodies of society are the biggest troublemakers.
Their 'must-save-the-world' attitude often disrupts the natural course, simply because they seek to enforce man-made ideas of what's good and evil.
An example is 'communism' which originally sprouted from a desire to change humanity for the better, based on equality and honest distribution of goods.
However, apart from the discussion if this approach is natural or not: the ways in which the communists spread their ideology were absolutely brutal.
In an ancient Chinese scripture, we find a story about a man named Yen Hui,

who asked Confucius for permission to travel to the country of Wei, after he heard that it's ruled by an incompetent ruler.

Yen Hui wanted to use everything he learned about governance, to improve the country of Wei. Confucius, however, discouraged him to do so.

Not only because Wei's highly disagreeable leader probably wouldn't listen, but also because people, in general, don't like outsiders coming in, telling what's better for them from a place of moral supremacy.

As Confucius stated:

"If you do not understand men's minds, but instead appear before a tyrant and force" him to listen to sermons on benevolence and righteousness, measures and standards – this is simply using other men's bad points to parade your own excellence."

We could ask ourselves: in what way is using other people's faults to create a nice role for ourselves, genuine virtue?

That's probably why so-called 'social justice warriors' are so hated.

We won't improve a situation by one-sidedly demonizing groups while placing ourselves on the moral high ground. This only creates more division, more tension, and will unlikely change things for the better in a sustainable man.

you want to rule the world and control it?
I don't think it can ever be done.
The world is a sacred vessel and it can not be controlled.
You will only make it worse if you try.
It may slip through your fingers and disappear.

Lao Tzu (Tao Te Ching),29

.

Now, the second one is...

Trying to be happy

No matter if it's the pursuit of money, status, fame, power, or knowledge; these ongoing efforts to be happy are the reason why we aren't.
We think that we're happy when we've got a million dollars in the bank or when we finally published that book or when our YouTube channels have a 1M subscribers, but this is hardly the case. Sure, we enjoy some momentary pleasure, but that's not happiness according to the ancient sages.
Moreover, by this pursuit, we exhaust our bodies and minds, while, tragically, never achieving what we're looking for.

This is what the world honours: wealth, eminence, long life, a good name. This is what the world finds happiness in: a life of ease, rich food, fine clothes, beautiful sights, sweet sounds.

This is what it looks down on: poverty, meanness, early death, a bad name. This is what it finds bitter: a life that knows no rest, a mouth that gets no rich food, no fine clothes for the body, no beautiful sights for the eye, no sweet sounds for the ear. People who can't get these things fret a great deal and are afraid - this is a stupid way to treat the body.

People who are rich wear themselves out rushing around on business, piling up more wealth than they could ever use - this is a superficial way to treat the body.

-Zhuangzi, 18-1

So, when chasing happiness is a blind alley, what should we do instead?
Before we get to the answers of this question.

Let's look at the third one

Trying to be something else

There is an ancient story about animals and the wind that envy each other for their in born characteristics.

"The centipede envies the snake for the fact that it can move without legs, but the snake envies the wind for its ability to travel great distances without having a body at all. However, the wind argues that it takes just a finger or foot to hinder it. All in all, nature has created everything with its own attributes".
Nothing is better than the other; only judgment makes it so.
Thus, we feel the need to change who we are, just to fit an ideal.
White-skinned people try to be tanned, while East-Asians try to look more European, Brunettes try to be blondes, and blondes try to be brunettes.
Also, we try to change ourselves because we want to conform to a manmade standard; to fit in, simply because we're seen as defects when we don't. -
So, a sixth' finger is cut off, just to comply with the five-finger standard.

Why can't we just be who we are, the way nature intended us to be?
That would be so much easier. Everyone and everything have its place in the whole. And by trying to alter this, we bring the world in disbalance.

When people see things as beautiful, ugliness is created.
When people see things as good, evil is created.
Being and non-being produce each other.
Difficult and easy complement each other.
Long and short define each other.
High and low oppose each other.
Fore and aft follow each other.
-Lao Tzu(Tao Te Ching),2

So, how can we put these ideas into practice?
The ancient sages suggest several things.

First of all, the spiritual masters suggest to the benefits of
taking the middle-path.

This means that we shouldn't stretch ourselves beyond our means, but stay cantered, so we conserve our health and stay close to our own nature.

"Follow the middle; go by what is constant, and you can stay in one piece, keep yourself
alive, look after your parents, and live out your years."

The ever-flowing 'energy of creation' is constant. And one who seeks it unlearns something new every day. So instead of limiting ourselves to a belief system, we let go, keep an open mind, and give the universe room to show itself as it is. Trying to change nature is a futile pursuit, as is trying to blur our vision of nature by man-made constructs.

Instead of adding to knowledge, we let go of knowledge, until we reach a point of inner stillness. Only then, we're opening ourselves up to that energy channel, or what we, from an atheistic point of view, could call God. In this state of emptiness, we feel content. And contentment is true happiness. The sages call this process the fasting of the heart. By unlearning something every day, we can arrive at non-action. It's the art of not trying.

Amor Fati

Amor fati means 'love of fate', and is a concept in Stoic philosophy but also in the works of Nietzsche. The idea is to love and embrace whatever the outcome is; no matter how hard we work towards a certain goal.

This way, we detach ourselves from possible results which enhances the ability to focus on the task at hand, and take away the anxiety that we may have concerning the future. The next question is of course: how can we do this?
In this chapter we will explore 4 ways to practise amor fati.
"Love of fate." The concept is simple; implementing it is more difficult because most minds drift off to the future very easily, and begin to fantasize about things that might happen. When we are restless because of the future, we either desire or averse a certain outcome. When we desire a certain outcome, the idea of not getting it makes us anxious. When we averse a certain outcome, the idea of incurring it makes us anxious.
Thus, it's the attachment to outcomes that creates the turmoil in our minds.
To solve this, Epictetus argues that we should remove desire and aversion in regards to things that are not in our control.

If you desire any of the things which are not in your own control, you must necessarily
be disappointed; and of those which are, and which it would be laudable to desire, nothing
is yet in your possession.
Use only the appropriate actions of pursuit and avoidance; and even these lightly, and
with gentleness and reservation.

> \-   Epictetus (Enchiridion)

Now this is easier said than done.
The Stoics believe that humans are naturally inclined to look for things that enhance their lives and avoid things that don't.
For example: we naturally look for wealth, healthy food, friendship, companionship, et cetera.

The Stoics called these things 'indifferent', that consist of preferred and dispreferred indifferent.
So, it's understandable that the prospect of losing or not obtaining certain preferred indifferent creates anxiety. The Stoics say, however, that these external factors are not necessary to be happy. Which is great news, because they are not in our control, so they would be very unreliable
sources of happiness. Nevertheless, many people worry endlessly about the future, that is the true reason behind unhappiness, we cause it by overthinking

about the outcomes. In order to reduce this maelstrom of anxious thoughts, trying to control the outcome is
pointless, because we can't. What we can control however, is the position we take towards the outcome, which the following
4 ways will be about.

Chapter 9

Purposefully expose yourself to the thing you averse.

Oftentimes, the things we averse are not as bad as we imagine them. Many people dread the idea of poverty for example, which isn't so strange because in current society we are constantly told that being poor is a terrible thing.

Someone fearing poverty might ask oneself: how can I possibly live without a 4-bedroom house, a car of a certain brand, two vacations a year, eating in a restaurant at least once
a week, and so on? The key to reduce the fear of certain outcomes, it to actually expose ourselves to them so we experience that a perceived negative outcome is not so bad. This way, we become familiar with hardship and, thus, prepared for it. I took (Fear of poverty) for mere example it doesn't mean that we all should start living in such ways.

It is precisely in times of immunity from care that the soul should toughen itself before hand
for occasions of greater stress, and it is while Fortune is kind that it should fortify
itself against her violence.
-    Lucius Annaeus Seneca

The ancient civilizations figured out that we do not need all these external things to be happy; **"happiness comes down to your own actions."**

So, when you fear poverty: how about living like a poor person for a number of days, in order to discover that being poor isn't so bad as we think?
Another common fear is the fear of being single and alone. When you're afraid of this, how about saying 'no' to relationships for a while, and
try to rely on yourself for happiness? Once we find out that being single actually can be great thing; we stop the fear of being alone once we are in a relationship.

This also prevents us from staying in abusive relationships, so we can take steps into the direction we want without fearing the consequences, and once we learn to start living happily with ourselves it is very easier to accept changes that comes with your partner and we are able to develop a sense of tolerance when we are inviting an unknown person in our personal
space.

Chapter 10

See change as an opportunity.

When I look back at life, I have seen that many things I feared actually came true. I have failed in many business, I have lost relationships, friends, family members and many opportunities. At the same time, I also got other things in return; as if life always tries to balance itself out. After I finished college, I was not able find a proper business idea.

The worst-case scenario happened: I had to try several different business ideas that were not what I wanted to do.
When I look back, the experiences I had during these years were absolutely life changing. I was able to do things and develop myself in certain ways, that I would never have done if my life turned out as I had previously hoped, and I'm happy things happened as they happened.

Don't demand that things happen as you wish, but wish that they happen as they do happen, and you will go on well.
- Epictetus (Enchiridion), 8

Yes, we fear losing our jobs, losing our marriage, losing our money.
But new situations, no matter how dreadful, always have new opportunities
hidden in them.

constant awareness that everything is born from change.
The knowledge that there is nothing nature loves more than to alter what exists
and make
new things like it.
All that exists is the seed of what will emerge from it.
-   Marcus Aurelius (Meditations), Book 4, 36

Chapter 11
Realize that happiness is relative.

In my early book (Happiness an analysis) I have discussed how happiness is adaptive. In 1978 there was a study by Brickman, Coates and Janoff-Bulman, who wanted to find out if happiness is relative.

In order to find that out, they studied a group of lottery winners, a group of paralyzed accident victims and a control group. Of course, we would expect that a lottery winner is much happier than someone who ended up paralyzed by an accident. And we also would expect that lottery winners are much happier than the control group, that didn't win the lottery but weren't paralyzed either.
In the first weeks or so, this was indeed the case.

But one year later, the controls and the lottery winners were equally happy, and only slightly happier than the paralyzed accident victims.
So, if happiness is relative: why should we fear the future?
The time and energy we spend on fearing the future is most likely worse than the future itself. A few years ago, my friend's uncle was diagnosed with cancer. At this moment he has been given up by the doctors which means that he might not see the new year.

When I asked my friend about his uncle recently, he told me that he feels fantastic. He enjoys life to the fullest and is grateful for every day that is given to him. So, what I learned from this incident, whatever tragedy happens: we know that the new circumstances never exclude a sense of happiness and wellbeing. Moreover, we might unexpectedly feel even better than before in the face of hardship. Hardship arrives in our lives always to teach us a different perspective towards life and many different situations. Instead of dreading the hardships and struggles we should embrace them and try to learn the lesson it is trying to teach us.

Chapter 12

Be in present

Now, the ways I have listed so far all have one thing in common: they point out that whatever, happens: we will cope with the new circumstances, whether it's good or bad (that depends upon our perspective towards it).

That we need the external things associated with our current life
 situation to be happy is an illusion; happiness is relative, as well as
unhappiness.
The future is just another path: not good, not bad; only if the mind makes it so.
Change is the very essence of life; resisting change is like resisting life.
As soon as we resist change, we're already in the future.

Don't be afraid of change
You may lose something good
But you may gain something better.

Because instead of accepting the present moment we try to preserve it for the days to come. Furthermore, we can say that there's no future nor is there a past.

There's only now, and that's why it is called "PRESENT."
When fate comes, it comes in the present.
That's why embracing fate can only be done in the present moment.
So, when the future hasn't arrived yet, why worry about it?
But when it comes, love it as it's here.
Love it before it's gone, because if you don't, you might regret that you didn't enjoy the moment when it was right before you.
Amor fati is the art of embracing whatever happens and not needing a single day beyond the present.
As Seneca wrote about Epicurus, who was tortured by painful diseases and said:

"To-day
And one other day have been the happiest of all!"

Abstract

A new book published by the author Prateek Tripathi "the project happiness"

Happiness is not something ready made. It comes from your own actions. This book is consisting of many real-life experiences and examples for better understanding.

He thinks most of us are familiar with the idea that we should simply 'act' and not 'try'. This idea is closely related to the 'flow-state'. To be so strong that nothing can disturb your peace of mind. To talk health, happiness, and prosperity to every person you meet. This book contains some ideas from great authors, poets and motivators like yen hui, Brickman, Coates and Janoff-Bulman...
An author Lucius Annaeus Seneca said that "It is precisely in times of immunity from care that the soul should toughen itself before hand
for occasions of greater stress, and it is while Fortune is kind that it should fortify itself against her violence."
This is an another example that shows how's this brilliant book contains many other great examples . this book will going to play an important role for motivations and suggests that what is good or bad.